KU-192-709

The
Fireside Book

A picture and a poem
for every mood
chosen by

David Hope

Printed and Published by
D. C. THOMSON & CO., LTD.
185 Fleet Street, London EC4A 2HS.
ISBN 0 85116 379 3

LAUGHTER

ALL along the highway
  I saw laughter—
As a cloud of blossomy trees,
Softly white and delicately rose—
Ripples of laughter
All over the hillside!

And under the tall tree trunks
I saw anemones—
Like a band of worshippers
With tiny hands
Stretched upward to the light
Amid a purple mist of violets.

Florence Irene Gubbins

CATLIKE

WHAT fun to be able to purr
    Loudly like her;
To respond to the stroking of fur
With this burr.

And then to be able to spit—
No wet, no hit—
But breathily to emit
Venom and wit.

Like her to be able to sleep,
Not just in a heap,
But elegantly keep
Secrets so deep.

To awake at the sound of a voice
Saying " Rejoice ".
To have such a wonderful choice
Of amorous boys.

To dote with pride as a mother,
Almost to smother
Sister and brother
In an overfond fluther.

In the end to forget
The whole suckling set
With no sort of fret
At once having met.

And loudly to purr
At the stroking of fur.
What fun to be her!

Kate Y. A. Bone

THE KISS

COME courting, sun—dispel
   The winter gloom;
Wake bud and flower to bloom:
Aspen and asphodel . . .
All that reflects God's grace
In soul and face!

Bring cuckoo in its mirth
With news of Spring,
Swallows that weave and wing
Through summer's youth;
Urchin and shy bank vole
From their dank hole!

Lovers that laugh and run
By woodland streams,
Who share each other's dreams;
Earth, sky and sun
Blending in the heart-bliss
Of one sweet kiss!

Edward Borland Ramsay

ELDORADO

GAILY bedight,
　　A gallant knight
　　　In sunshine and in shadow
Had journeyed long,
Singing a song,
　　　In search of Eldorado.

But he grew old,
This knight so bold,
　　　And o'er his heart a shadow
Fell, as he found
No spot of ground
　　　That looked like Eldorado.

And, as his strength
Failed him at length,
　　　He met a pilgrim shadow.
" Shadow," said he,
" Where can it be,
　　　This land of Eldorado?"

" Over the Mountains
Of the Moon,
　　　Down the valley of the Shadow,
Ride, boldly ride,"
The shade replied,
　　　" If you seek for Eldorado."

Edgar Allan Poe

THE FARM OF THE APPLE TREE

I SAW you standing by the gate,
  I heard you call to me
With the wind cry and the bird cry and the
  far-off cry of the sea.
Was there fire in your eyes that they could light
Such fire in the heart of me,
When the young moon sailed from amber clouds
O'er the Farm of the Apple Tree?

A light from the window flashed and leapt
Through the night in a golden stream,
With the moonfire and the starfire and the fire
  of a world a-dream;
But I only saw your burning eyes
Implore me silently,
And felt your hands upon my own
By the Farm of the Apple Tree.

You woke the life within my life,
My soul from her sleep of years.
You lighted a lamp in the World for me that
  is blinding my eyes with tears,
But you left me a dream I cannot lose
Of fire in the heart of me,
And the touch of your hands upon my own
In the Farm of the Apple Tree.

Joan Rundall

CAT'S CRADLE

ALTHOUGH it has a jolly name,
Cat's cradle is a funny game—
I like to play it all the same.

It's easy when you first begin,
But when it goes all long and thin
I daren't put my fingers in.

If mother's anywhere about
We stand against the door and shout
Until she comes and helps us out.

Her fingers look so long and white,
Her rings are very sparkly bright,
She *almost always* gets it right.

Rose Fyleman

A COUNTRY SUNDAY

IT'S very quiet and still.
  In the lane
There is no rumble of carts,
  Over at the farm
No boom of the threshing-mill.
It's Sunday morning again.

The folk are all in bed resting
—Taking a longer lie—
  By-and-by
They'll get up leisurely and dress,
And after they've fed the hens and the cattle
  and all,
They'll go up to church at the call
  Of the bell, to bless
  God for His gifts.
  (Watch how the sunlight shifts
  From face to face along the pews.)

Homeward again in little groups of threes and
  twos
  To dinner and a sleep; and then maybe
  A pot of tea
  And a stroll—two by two—
  Up the lane.
  Overhead in the blue
The quiet stars return. Far off up the hill
The evening bell sounds alternately soft and shrill
  —Carried and withdrawn;
  From cottage roofs the smoke
Goes up awhile straightly into the night;
At last, behind the yellow blinds, the light
  Is suddenly gone.
  Sunday is over again until next week.

Isobel W. Hutchison

BY THE RIVER

BLUE fire on green, the kingfisher
   Skims flashing o'er the river
Where, rainbow-winged, a dragonfly,
   Like diamond brooch a-shiver,
Alights on heady meadowsweet
   Beside the trampled sedge;
Sheer beauty blossoms at the feet
   And round the water's edge.

Blue fire on green in amber light,
   Veined gossamer on cream,
The golden sequins on opaque
   And softly-whispering stream
Are precious gifts that all may share,
   A cornucopia fair,
Descanting crimson, peach, and gold
   O'er wild-rose scented air.

Violet Hall

LOVE SONG

I MADE another song,
  In likeness of my love,
And sang it all day long,
  Around, beneath, above;
I told my secret out,
That none might be in doubt.

I sang it to the sky,
  That veiled his face to hear
How far her azure eye
  Outdoes his splendid sphere;
But at her eyelids' name
His white clouds fled for shame.

I told it to the trees,
  And to the flowers confessed,
And said not one of these
  Is like my lily dressed;
Nor spathe nor petal dared
Vie with her body bared.

I shouted to the sea
  That set his waves a-prance;
Her floating hair is free,
  Free are her feet to dance;
And for thy wrath, I swear
Her frown is more to fear.

And as in happy mood
  I walked and sang alone,
At eve beside the wood
  I met my love, my own,
And sang to her the song
I had sung all day long.

Robert Bridges

HOW FLOWERS GROW

THIS is how the flowers grow:
   I have watched them and I know.

First, above the ground is seen
A tiny blade of purest green,
Reaching up and peeping forth
East and West, and South and North.

Then it shoots up day by day,
Curling in a curious way
Round a blossom, which it keeps
Warm and cosy while it sleeps.

And when birds begin to sing
Of the balmy breath of Spring,
And the clouds in Summer's quest
All come sailing from the West;

Then the sunbeams find their way
To the sleeping bud and say,
" We are children of the sun
Sent to wake thee, little one."

And the leaflet, opening wide,
Shows the tiny bud inside,
Peeping with half-opened eye
On the bright and sunny sky.

Breezes from the West and South
Lay their kisses on its mouth;
Till the petals are all grown,
And the bud's a flower full-blown.

That is how the flowers grow:
I have watched them and I know.

Gabriel Setoun

HOPES AND DREAMS

YOU come to me upon my dreams
    Like a white sail on twilight seas,
Or as a moving music seems
To swim on silence to its close.
My hopes—how far you pass from those!
My dreams—how sure you are of these!

All things are novel since love came;
Through the dim chapel of my heart
You walk with ministering flame
To light the candles of surprise.
My hopes—how teach them to be wise?
My dreams—how bid them to depart?

The thought of you is swift and strange
To find me out—because of you
I think my very self shall change,
And grow in tune with what you are.
My hopes—are they indeed so far?
My dreams—shall they perhaps come true?

Gerald Gould

THE LOVE LESSON

"I WILL give you gowns of silk,
    A soft-eyed pony, white as milk,
Jewels glowing, none more fine:
Will you place your hand in mine?"

" *Silk against the skin is cold,*
The sweetest pony must grow old;
Jewels, too, I shall decline:
I will not place my hand in thine!"

" You shall have a mansion fair,
And a maid to dress your hair,
Ships to venture o'er the brine:
Will you change your name to mine?"

" A mansion fair is not for me;
A maid and I would ne'er agree;
No ship launched on Clyde or Tyne
Will make me change my name to thine!"

" All my wealth lies at your feet,
But no further I'll entreat;
Prithee tell me, ere we part:
Is there a gateway to your heart?"

" Wealth and power, what are those?
Hearts surrender to a rose.
Love which seeks to understand
Will find the way to win my hand!"

Peter Cliffe

THE CALL

OH I must away from the city's din,
   For I would refresh once more
Where the opal seas come sweeping in
   To a dreamy palm-fringed shore;
For I long to stand on foam-flecked sand
   While the scented breezes blow,
And it's there I'll find that peace of mind
   Where the bright hibiscus grow.

I am weary now of the throbbing street
   With its arid dusty pall,
Let me trade the sound of hurrying feet
   For the sea-bird's lonely call.
Oh, what joy is found if my heart resound
   With that stirring note again—
Every care's aground when outward bound
   For the ports across the main.

'Tis the only life I languish for,
   'Tis the only one I'll own
When I'm far beyond the harbour bar
   And the in-shore lights have gone.
Then before the mast, let the wind rave past,
   And ride o'er the avid deep;
Though the call's the last, my soul's steadfast
   Where the darling dolphins sleep.

Edward Borland Ramsay

MAY SONG

O LOVELY May,
  In all your beauty singing!
All laughter in your fair array
  Of bridal blossoms, ringing
The bluebells in the woodland. Stay
  Your fragrant whiteness and waylay
  The hours with pleading beauty.

  Pray
The winds to fold their pinions
  Lest they bruise
  Your delicate laces. O delay
The fall of petals that would spill
Their sweetness for the breeze to lay
A dainty carpet for the feet of June,
  That to the piping tune
  Of cuckoos comes too soon!

Florence Irene Gubbins

STOLEN MOMENTS

I SIT lost among the silver-swaying grasses
  In a lullaby of gentle rustling sound,
And I listen to the water wimple past me,
See a lush and living greenness all around;
Small brown butterflies dance private petronellas
In, round and through the slender bending stems,
Briars that are peopled by white earth stars
Offer the Summer sun their petalled gems;
Bees burrow in rich cream of meadow sweetness
That throws hot syrup scent into the air,
And I know that, powder-fine, the bloom is blowing,
That a mist of unseen silk drifts everywhere.

Stolen fruit and stolen moments have more flavour,
And soon I must return to kitchen sink,
Sure that life for me will never lose its savour—
As long as sometimes, I can drowse and dream and think.

Margaret Gillies Brown

GRANIA

SHE leaned out over the low half-door
   and she waved to me
   as we went by.
Her dark hair shone, and her eyes
   were as clear as the sky—
And for me, in that place time stopped
   'til the day I die.

Year upon year has gone past
since that summer noon
   when she smiled to me there;
But still in my heart we are young
   and the day is fair:
And still she leans over the door,
   with the sun on her hair.

Sydney Bell

ONCE UPON A TIME

BEFORE the stars were numbered,
    My proud Halcyone,
We lived our gipsy life beside
    A burning Eastern sea,
With fisherfolk and sailorfolk
    As happy as could be.

And I, your dark-haired lover,
    Would sail at break of day,
To dive for clustered shell-fish
    Beneath the shimmering bay,
And pearls and purples to adorn
    Princesses far away.

And you would speak with strangers,
    Sweet-tongued Halcyone,
With solemn Syrian merchants,
    And Greeks from oversea,
And travellers with golden tales
    And eyes of mystery.

Then would we entertain them
    With simple island fare
And barter all my long day's toil
    For coloured earthenware,
And one great gleaming ruby
    To smoulder in your hair.

And they would praise your beauty
    With grave and courtly speech,
Smile in their beards and leave us
    Like children, each to each,
Whose love held more of wisdom
    Than all their lore could teach.

P. Hugh B. Lyon

TO A CUCKOO

STRANGE bird, where is your presence found?
  In solemn keep, or woodland gay?
Or does each echo but resound
  Through sylvan scenes of yesterday?

Such phantom pleadings I have heard
  When wand'ring as a happy boy:
'Twas then I called you foolish bird
  That courted every infant ploy.

But I have learned to love you more
  With each brief visit which you give;
And though your customs I deplore,
  I offer you a rich reprieve!

For time has wisely tutor'd me
  That when the other lands you wing,
You leave within my memory,
  The joys of an eternal Spring.

Edward Borland Ramsay

SUN AND RAIN

I HAVE found the way to the gates of heaven
　　Where the streets are paved with gold,
And the smoke and grime have fled away
　　As the sound of a tale that is told.

For lo! I stand on the sea of glass
　　And the secret things are plain
In the crowded ways of a London street,
　　Where the sun has kissed the rain!

Florence Irene Gubbins

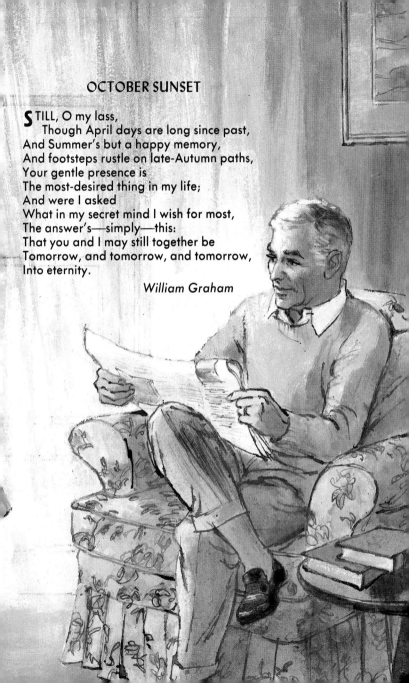

OCTOBER SUNSET

STILL, O my lass,
    Though April days are long since past,
And Summer's but a happy memory,
And footsteps rustle on late-Autumn paths,
Your gentle presence is
The most-desired thing in my life;
And were I asked
What in my secret mind I wish for most,
The answer's—simply—this:
That you and I may still together be
Tomorrow, and tomorrow, and tomorrow,
Into eternity.

William Graham

HURRYINGS

THE sea seemed in a hurry today,
  Polished to silver by a craftsman sun.
Why should it scurry, hurry? It is governed—
And will return.

The sky seemed in a hurry today,
Bustling cumulus crowds off to the game.
Why should they churn and turn? They will come
  again—
Much the same.

The boy seemed in a hurry today,
Running a damp sand band on the edge of time.
Why should he race and pace? His creel of years
  waits—
Unlike mine.

Hamish Brown

CORNERS

I AM a constant corner sitter, I
　Like the right-angled privacy of nooks
Where trusted friends immortalise themselves
In books beside me on my corner shelves.
　　A book, a cigarette, a drink, a cat,
　　What corner could be better than all that?

I am a further corner sitter, I
Like the delight of sitting in the sun.
Here there are blackbirds, pausing in their search,
A mist of greenness climbs upon the larch.
　　A flower, a bird, the humming of a bee,
　　These make a sheltered sanctuary for me.

I am a constant corner sitter, I
Like the right-angled privacy of nooks.

Kate Y. A. Bone

ON PANCAKE HILL

I WAS a boy, and you were fair;
   Ah, summer days so warm and still!
    We roamed the fields without a care,
Until we came to Pancake Hill.

The buttercups spilled fairy gold;
    We dipped our fingers in the rill.
A lark its lilting legends told
    And hours were sweet on Pancake Hill.

Fluffy clouds went drifting slow,
    Above the ruined water-mill;
A gentle breeze began to blow
    And stir the grass on Pancake Hill.

Ah, dearest, time flits by too soon,
    And Summer yields to Autumn's chill.
Do you recall that afternoon
    When we were young on Pancake Hill?

Peter Cliffe

STORM CLOUDS

NOW overhead the rooks are flying low,
　　They stagger, fighting hard against the gale,
And call with raucous voices surging loud,
　　As on they press with strength that will not fail.

The winter afternoon frowns darkly down,
　　And spectre-like the barren naked trees
Toss to and fro their arms athwart the sky,
　　As if in search of prey which they might seize.

The storm increases; tempests sweep the woods,
　　And bend the crested plumes of ancient pines,
Yet for a moment scudding clouds reveal
　　The evening star behind—which tranquil shines.

Edith A. Vassie

THE COUNTRY HOUSE

THERE are the old house and the leafy garden
    And the long Summer full of the sound of
      bees,
The lazy swing of lace at the open windows,
    The drowsy hammock under the chestnut trees.

There the white promise of the flowering orchard,
    The glow of borders beside the level lawns,
The gentleness of rain in the velvet evenings,
    The benison of birds in the shining dawns.

There the slow afternoons of scented silence;
    Only at intervals the rhythm of hoofs
Alone on the dusty road and soon departed;
    The languor of sunlight over the quiet roofs.

There the old tales to keep a child enchanted,
    The hours of coloured fancy and idle bliss,
Content that asks no dearer delight than being,
    No sweeter breath, no happier heart than this.

And there he walks in spirit far from the tumult
    Of these wild years, and sees bright visions
      burn
In that alluring land of the unforgotten
    To which he dreams that his days may yet
      return.

Nancy Firkins

ROMANCE

I SAW a ship a-sailing,
   A-sailing on the sea;
Her masts were of the shining gold,
   Her deck of ivory;
And sails of silk, as soft as milk,
   And silvern shrouds had she.

And round about her sailing,
   The sea was sparkling white,
The waves all clapped their hands and sang
   To see so fair a sight.
They kissed her twice, they kissed her thrice,
   And murmured with delight.

Then came the gallant captain,
   And stood upon the deck;
In velvet coat, and ruffles white,
   Without a spot or speck;
And diamond rings, and triple strings
Of pearls around his neck.

And four-and-twenty sailors
   Were round him bowing low;
On every jacket three times three
   Gold buttons in a row;
And cutlasses down to their knees;
   They made a goodly show.

And then the ship went sailing,
   A-sailing o'er the sea;
She dived beyond the setting sun,
   But never back came she,
For she found the lands of the golden sands,
   Where the pearls and diamonds be.

Gabriel Setoun

A DEVON MEMORY

THERE was an afternoon of high sweet wind,
   Of fretted lace upon a sapphire sea,
Of flowers red and gold, and sunlit grass
     Where danced the shade of every swaying
     tree.

There was an afternoon of quiet rooms,
  Old books, old lore, old Persian pottery,
Of cheerful talk and silence understood,
  And amber honey in the comb for tea.

Fate, you have darts! Life, you have pains
  unknown!
  We shall remember that you have been kind;
When, from our lips the very breath was blown,
  Then, on that afternoon of high sweet wind.

Mabel V. Irvine

HIPS

DOWN on the river-bank today
   I saw a bush of scarlet hips
Just at the place where the water slips
Under the willows, the willows grey,
Under the willows and then away,
Away to the sea and the ships!

The sky was misty and dark when I saw
That bush of hips by the river's brim,
And the wilted grasses were damp and dim
And the mournful rook in the wood called long
At the head of his mournful sanhedrim. *
But the hips looked up and laughed at him
Suddenly, like a song.

Isobel W. Hutchison

* court, council.

A PORTRAIT

WITHIN her eyes of gray
   Such haunting sadness lies,
Around her lips doth play
A little smile midway,
   Yet tinged with faint surprise.

The soft and shadowy hair
   Strays with a tender grace,
Caressing here and there,
With an elusive care,
   The ivory-tinted face.

Time, with the sculptor's art,
   Hath moulded undefined
Vague longings of the heart,
Or lingered to impart
   Vain strivings of the mind.

Some sleeping question yet
   Unanswered doth remain,
With touch of dim regret,
That none was ever met
   To answer or explain.

And thus her eyes of gray
   Their haunting sadness keep,
For tears shed yesterday
Have left a memory
   Of thoughts, for tears too deep.

Anne MacDonald

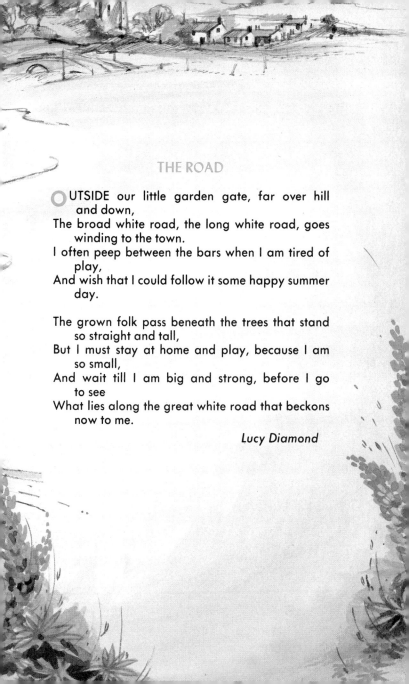

THE ROAD

OUTSIDE our little garden gate, far over hill
and down,
The broad white road, the long white road, goes
winding to the town.
I often peep between the bars when I am tired of
play,
And wish that I could follow it some happy summer
day.

The grown folk pass beneath the trees that stand
so straight and tall,
But I must stay at home and play, because I am
so small,
And wait till I am big and strong, before I go
to see
What lies along the great white road that beckons
now to me.

Lucy Diamond

LAMENT

WHERE once we waited for the train,
  Beside the station-master's flowers,
Now ruinous in wind and rain
  The station dreams away the hours.

Tall grass and ragwort flourish rank
  Where ran the broad and shining rails;
Above the rusting water tank,
  The rook, a heedless pirate, sails.

And yet, when autumn nights are still,
  And I can't sleep, why do I seem
To hear a whistle blowing shrill
  That mourns the golden days of steam?

Peter Cliffe

INTERLUDE

WE lost our tempers in the lane
  And angry words went flying.
We vowed we'd never meet again,
  And then she started crying.

She took the glove from off her hand,
  The ring from off her finger,
And coldly said: " I understand—
  You really needn't linger!"

The sun found gold-dust in her hair,
  The day was so beguiling,
That still I hesitated there,
  Until we started smiling.

Our foolish quarrel fled away;
  How much I would have missed her!
We talked about our wedding day—
  But not before I'd kissed her.

Peter Cliffe

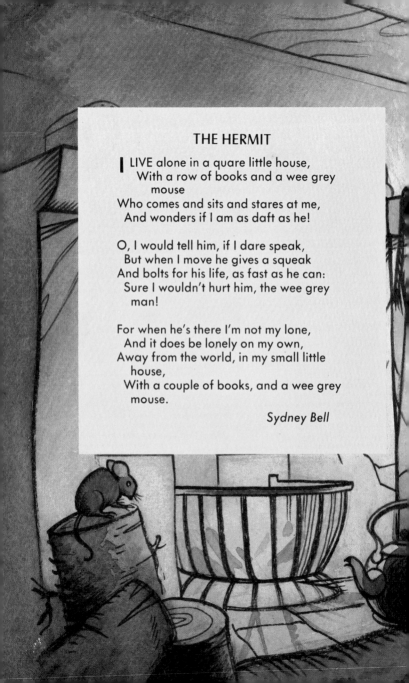

THE HERMIT

I LIVE alone in a quare little house,
  With a row of books and a wee grey
    mouse
Who comes and sits and stares at me,
  And wonders if I am as daft as he!

O, I would tell him, if I dare speak,
  But when I move he gives a squeak
And bolts for his life, as fast as he can:
  Sure I wouldn't hurt him, the wee grey
    man!

For when he's there I'm not my lone,
  And it does be lonely on my own,
Away from the world, in my small little
    house,
  With a couple of books, and a wee grey
    mouse.

Sydney Bell

IT'S COMING

THE wind's getting ready,
   With hustle and bustle,
To whip round the trees
   And make the leaves rustle;
To colour them tawny
   And colour them brown—
The trees in the country
   And trees in the town.
The time's looming nearer,
   With golden leaves falling,
Tho' Autumn is with us,
   It's Winter-time calling;
With rubies in hedgerows
   Of haws and of hips,
And last of the berries
   That purple the lips.
The rose is still lovely
   In spite of the tussle
With wind and the rain,
   And the hustle and bustle;
With pearls on her petals
   And damp of the mist
Where cool of the morning
   And night-time have kissed.

Violet Hall

IT'S COMING

THE wind's getting ready,
　　With hustle and bustle,
To whip round the trees
　　And make the leaves rustle;
To colour them tawny
　　And colour them brown—
The trees in the country
　　And trees in the town.
The time's looming nearer,
　　With golden leaves falling,
Tho' Autumn is with us,
　　It's Winter-time calling;
With rubies in hedgerows
　　Of haws and of hips,
And last of the berries
　　That purple the lips.
The rose is still lovely
　　In spite of the tussle
With wind and the rain,
　　And the hustle and bustle;
With pearls on her petals
　　And damp of the mist
Where cool of the morning
　　And night-time have kissed.

Violet Hall

HAVE come home again, and softlier
  Breathes the Spring's cold and
    wintry-seeming air.
I shall not hear the thundering traffic roar
Up the grey hill of Knightsbridge any more,
Nor hear the brakes of scarlet buses scream
As I slip over into sleep from dream.
But I shall hear the envious restless sea
Under my window calling " Home!" to me,
And sea-birds swinging on that trackless deep
Cry to me from their windy ways, " Sleep, sleep!"
All through the night the London lights may shine
And raucous voices from the street uprise,
My heart is quiet as I close my eyes
And still and velvet-dark the room now mine.

Mabel V. Irvine

HARVEST

THE budding was all for this,
   The blackbird's bliss
In May began it,
And did fan it
Into this fire.
June's delicate desire
Was towards this high attainment, and this boon
Of perfect noon,
—The ripened ear—the plum ready to fall
From the warm south wall.

For this was all the love
That late did move
The plumy cherry.
Ah! she was very
Joyous indeed
For thought of this, the seed.
And even for this, in early days of March
Before the larch,
The aproned sower paced across the land
With floury hand.

Isobel W. Hutchison

DUET TO AN ISLAND COUPLE

HIS heart belongs to the lonely places,
   The empty shore where the strong tide races,
Rock-rising walls where wild combers break,
The gale and the gull and the kittiwake;
Fresh greening earth, low clouding skies,
Moor-mist and rain and the rainbow rise,
Sun's late fall on a midsummer night,
Strangeness and silence, miraculous light;
His heart belongs to the lonely places
To a weathered people with ancient faces.

Her heart belongs to the far-off places,
An island wrapped in the sea's embraces,
Where waves in the caves eddying round
Boom with an organ's unstoppered sound;
The violin bow and its poignant tune,
Warm island voices soft at noon;
The ceilidh held in the peat fire glow,
The lilting song and the lively tow;
Her heart belongs to the far-off places,
An island wrapped in the sea's embraces.

Margaret Gillies Brown

VICTORIAN MISS

CHARLOTTE Harriet Emily May,
   A sweet little girl in a far off day:
From her side-button boots
To her bonneted crown,
Long loose ringlets tumbling down,
She had an air demure yet pert,
A sash at her waist
And a muslin-sprigged skirt
Over petticoats frilled
In flannel and lawn
With a pintucked bodice
As once was worn.

Up to bed by candlelight
In her nightgown flounced and white,
She knelt in prayer as children ought
Remembering all she had been taught;
Then she climbed into her bed,
Rag curlers bobbing on her head,
And gazed in wonder at the moon
Floating, she thought, like a white balloon,
And Charlotte Harriet Emily May
Could scarcely wait for the break of day.

Barbara Gray Jemison

A CHILD'S SONG

ONCE I was a little bird,
    And when the bells were ringing
In the quiet eventide—
    You may have heard me singing.

Once I was a little bee,
    A careless, lazy rover,
And many pleasant days I spent
    Among the creamy clover.

Then I was a little breeze,
    I ruffled curtain laces,
I kissed, and left the dreamy smiles
    On sleeping baby faces.

But now I am a little sigh,
    And dull grey days express me.
Oh, when you hear me passing by
    Just ask the Lord to bless me.

So that I may become a smile,
    With bright blue skies above me,
I'll flicker on your lips awhile,
    And everyone will love me.

Gloria Rawlinson

SEPTEMBER

THERE are twelve months throughout the year,
    From January to December—
And the primest month of all the twelve
    Is the merry month of September.
        Then apples so red
        Hang overhead,
        And nuts ripe-brown
        Come showering down
In the bountiful days of September.

There are flowers enough in the Summer-time,
    More flowers than I can remember—
But none with the purple, gold, and red
    That dye the flowers of September,
    The gorgeous flowers of September!
        And the sun looks through
        A clearer blue,
        And the moon at night
        Sheds a clearer light
On the beautiful flowers of September.

Mary Howitt

THE LAMP-LIGHTER

MY tea is nearly ready and the sun has left the
sky;
It's time to take the window to see Leerie going
by;
For every night at tea-time and before you take
your seat,
With lantern and with ladder he comes posting
up the street.

Now Tom would be a driver and Maria go to sea,
And my papa's a banker and as rich as he can
be;
But I, when I am stronger and can choose what
I'm to do,
O, Leerie, I'll go round at night and light the lamps
with you.

For we are very lucky, with a lamp before the
door;
And Leerie stops to light it as he lights so many
more;
And oh! before you hurry by with ladder and with
light,
O, Leerie, see a little child and nod to him to-night!

Robert Louis Stevenson

AUTUMN IN GLENPROSEN

HERE buzzard and blackcock
    With grey-feathered feet,
Here mountain and river
    And landscape all meet;
Beyond the arched rainbow
    On this narrow way,
October's bright shoes
    Have crept lightly today;
Soft colours imposed
    On a sepia print,
Of bleak barren Winter
    No skeletal hint.
Beeches and birches
    In sun-enthralled gold
Find russet of bracken,
    Its greenness grown old,
And lonely grey houses
    Half-hidden by hill
With smoke signals leaping,
    All other things still . . .

Past Summer's high rainbow
    I cannot yet see,
But I hope that, as gently,
    The Autumn finds me.

Margaret Gillies Brown

THE SINGING WIND

THE wind went singing over the hill,
  Down by the river and up by the mill;
The wind went singing over my head
And never a solemn word it said.

Never a word, but a singing sound
That sent the brown sails swinging round—
Free, free, free, and away they sped—
The singing wind and a sheaf of bread.

Across the meadow, beyond the down,
The wind went singing over the town;
Over the town and away again
Singing the song of countrymen.

Singing the song of the open wold,
The wind blew shrill, and the wind blew cold;
The wind went singing over my head
And never a solemn word it said.

Edward Borland Ramsay

WADING

SUMMER'S sunny days have come;
    Soft and sweet the wind is blowing;
Bees across the meadow hum
    Where the golden flowers are growing;
Fields and trees are green and fair,
And sunshine's sleeping everywhere.

O, the sunny Summer days,
    When the ripples dance and quiver;
And the sun at noontide lays
    Star-like jewels on the river!
Take your shoes off; wade in here
Where the water's warm and clear.

Listen to the song it sings,
    Ever rippling, ever flowing;
Telling of a thousand things;
    Whence it comes, and whither going;
Singing, like the birds and bees,
Of the wondrous world it sees.

See the fishes dart about,
    Where a thousand lights are dancing;
Here a minnow, there a trout,
    Like a sword of silver glancing.
Is it hide-and-seek they play
Through the sunny Summer day?

All the wood is filled with sound,
    And the very air is ringing,
Up and down and all around,
    With the songs the birds are singing.
O, the golden Summer hours,
When earth's a paradise of flowers!

Gabriel Setoun

THE QUARREL

I QUARRELLED with my brother,
 I don't know what about,
One thing led to another,
 And somehow we fell out.
The start of it was slight,
 The end of it was strong,
He said he was right,
 I knew he was wrong!

We hated one another,
 The afternoon turned black,
Then suddenly my brother
 Thumped me on the back
And said, " Oh, come along!
 We can't go on all night—
I was in the wrong."
 So he was in the right.

Eleanor Farjeon

THE ROAD TO NOWHERE

OVER the Sally Gap into Wicklow,
  The mountains sunbaked and the turf crackin':
Thinkin' of Donegal or smoky Aran,
  And I walkin' on the Road to Nowhere.

A pipe in me teeth, I nearin' Bantry,
The sea like a sheet of steel or blue silver;
At the back o' me mind a girl in Sligo,
  And I walkin' on the Road to Nowhere.

A couple o' pints in a pub in Galway;
A couple o' trout from the Corrib river;
Thoughts of Rostrevor and maybe of Rathlin,
  And I walkin' on the Road to Nowhere.

Crows by the thousand flappin' over Derry;
A stick in me hand from the wood of Croaghan:
Blues in Connemara, Errigal before me—
  And I walkin' on the Road to Nowhere!

Sydney Bell

AFTER THE DROUGHT

SUDDENLY the wind turned to the west;
  The heat abated;
In came the rain from the sea,
So long awaited,
And everywhere the seaweed smell
Swept o'er the land. In gusty haste
The driving rain
Made rivers in the dry and dusty road;
Under the swift-cloud sky,
The trees and flowers and ground
Were fresh and sweet.
After long days of arid, burning heat,
All summer's beauty was re-born again
In the driving, drenching miracle of the rain!

Aileen E. Passmore

WINTER

CLOUDED with snow
  The cold winds blow,
And shrill on leafless bough
The robin with its burning breast
  Alone sings now.

The rayless sun,
  Day's journey done,
Sheds its last ebbing light
On fields in leagues of beauty spread
  Unearthly white.

Thick draws the dark,
  And spark by spark,
The frost-fires kindle, and soon
Over that sea of frozen foam,
  Floats the white moon.

Walter de la Mare

PANSIES

SOFT as a silence, tender as a dream,
  Elusive as some scarce remembered theme,
Fragrant with memory of joys we knew,
Pansies for thoughts, yea, thoughts I send to you.

Pansies for thoughts! Purple, methinks for sorrow;
Golden for glory, in some sweet tomorrow;
Blue—faith and constancy to lovers send,
White, for that peace which cometh in the end.

Today these pansies with my love I send—
Fragrant with thoughts of one I call my friend,
Petals all golden, purple, white and blue,
Pansies for thoughts, and all are thoughts of you.

Anne MacDonald

THE KERNEL

NOW that the flush of summer is gone,
　　And in the lane no flower is seen,
　No hedge in leaf,
No tree in gold or green;

Now that the golden fruit is stored,
And in the wood no song is heard,
　No merry stir
Of song from any bird;

Now that the uncompanioned wind
Blows cold across the naked land,
　And, hung in black,
Bare trees like mourners stand;

Winter reveals through falling rain,
A strength which summer had left unseen:
　Beauty and peace
Which, but for tears, had been in vain,
Which, but for loss, had never been.

Frank Kendon

ACKNOWLEDGMENTS

Our thanks to the Society of Authors and the Literary Trustees of Walter de la Mare for "Winter"; to David Higham Associates Ltd for "The Quarrel" by Eleanor Farjeon; to Methuen Children's Books Ltd for "Cat's Cradle" by Rose Fyleman; to Charles Griffiths for "After the Drought" by Aileen Passmore; to Mrs Celia Kendon for "The Kernel" by Frank Kendon; to Kate Y.A. Bone for "Catlike" and "Corners"; to Edward Borland Ramsay for "The Kiss", "The Call", "To a Cuckoo" and "The Singing Wind"; to Violet Hall for "By the River" and "It's Coming"; to Peter Cliffe for "The Love Lesson", "On Pancake Hill", "Lament", and "Interlude"; to Margaret Gillies Brown for "Stolen Moments", "Duet to an Island Couple" and "Autumn in Glen Prosen"; to Sydney Bell for "Grania", "The Hermit" and "The Road to Nowhere"; to P. Hugh B. Lyon for "Once Upon a Time"; to William Graham for "October Sunset"; to Hamish Brown for "Hurryings"; to Barbara Gray Jemison for "Victorian Miss".